Jesus is Coming Back.

Get Ready!

Walgenia George Morgan

Archway Publishing books may be ordered through booksellers or by contacting:

Archway Publishing
1663 Liberty Drive
Bloomington, IN 47403
www.archwaypublishing.com
844-669-3957

ISBN: 978-1-6657-3561-2 (sc)
ISBN: 978-1-6657-3562-9 (hc)
ISBN: 978-1-6657-3560-5 (e)

Library of Congress Control Number: 2022923650

Print information available on the last page.

Archway Publishing rev. date: 04/26/2023

Jesus is Coming Back. *Get Ready!*

Forward

"Beloved, I now write this second epistle... that scoffers will come in the last days, walking according to their own lusts, and saying, "Where is the promise of His coming? For since the fathers fell asleep, all things continue as *they were* from the beginning of creation." For this they willfully forget: that by the word of God the heavens were of old, and the earth standing out of water and in the water, by which the world *that* then existed perished, being flooded with water. But the heavens and the earth *which* are now preserved by the same word, are reserved for fire until the day of judgment and perdition of ungodly men."

"But, beloved, do not forget this one thing, that with the Lord one day *is* as a thousand years, and a thousand years as one day. The Lord is not slack concerning *His* promise, as some count slackness, but is longsuffering toward us, not willing that any should perish but that all should come to repentance."

"But the day of the Lord will come as a thief in the night, in which the heavens will pass away with a great noise, and the elements will melt with fervent heat; both the earth and the works that are in it will be burned up. Therefore, since all these things will be dissolved, what manner *of persons* ought you to be in holy conduct and godliness, looking for and hastening the coming of the day of God, because of which the heavens will be dissolved, being on fire, and the elements will melt with fervent heat?" 2 Peter 3 vs 1-12 NKJV

"God who at various times and in various ways spoke in time past to the fathers by the prophets, has in these last days spoken to us by His Son, who He has appointed heir of all things, through whom He also made the worlds." Hebrews 1 vs 1-2. NKJV

Make Jesus your Lord and Savior

Jesus is Coming Back

WHO IS JESUS?

In Christianity, Jesus is the Son of God and the second person in the Trinity. Jesus was born of the Virgin Mary, a Jewish teenager in Bethlehem of Judea, a city south of Jerusalem, Israel. Jesus' birth was foretold 11 times in the Old Testament by prophets. For example, in the book of Isaiah chapter 9 verse 6 we read:

"For unto us a Child is born, unto us a Son is given, and the government shall be upon His shoulder and His name shall be called Wonderful, Counselor, The Mighty God, the Everlasting father, the Prince of Peace."

According to the Bible, the genealogy of Jesus is as follows:

Abraham was the
        father of Isaac,
    Isaac the father
        of Jacob,
    Jacob the father

of Judah and
his brothers,
Judah the father of
Perez and Zerah,
whose mother
was Tamar,
Perez the father
of Hezron,
Hezron the father
of Ram,
Ram the father of
Amminadab,
Amminadab the father
of Nahshon,
Nahshon the father
of Salmon,
Salmon the father of
Boaz, whose mother
was Rahab,
Boaz the father
of Obed, whose
mother was Ruth,
Obed the father
of Jesse,

and Jesse the father
of King David.
David was the father of
Solomon, whose
mother had been
Uriah's wife,
Solomon the father
of Rehoboam,
Rehoboam the father
of Abijah,
Abijah the father
of Asa,
Asa the father of
Jehoshaphat,
Jehoshaphat the
father of Jehoram,
Jehoram the father
of Uzziah,
Uzziah the father
of Jotham,
Jotham the father
of Ahaz,
Ahaz the father of
Hezekiah,

Hezekiah the father
  of Manasseh,
Manasseh the father
  of Amon,
Amon the father
  of Josiah,
 and Josiah the father
  of Jeconiah and
  his brothers at
  the time of the
  exile to Babylon.
 After the exile
  to Babylon:
Jeconiah was the
  father of Shealtiel,
Shealtiel the father
  of Zerubbabel,
Zerubbabel the father
  of Abihud,
Abihud the father
  of Eliakim,
Eliakim the father
  of Azor,

Azor the father
of Zadok,
Zadok the father
of Akim,
Akim the father
of Elihud,
Elihud the father
of Eleazar,
Eleazar the father
of Matthan,
Matthan the father
of Jacob,
and Jacob the father
of Joseph, the
husband of Mary,
and Mary was the
mother of Jesus
who is called the
Messiah. Matthew
1 vs 1-16. NIV

Make Jesus your Lord and Savior

At His birth two people testified of Jesus's coming to earth and its meaning:

"And behold there was a man in Jerusalem whose name was Simeon, and the same man was just and devout waiting for the consolation of Israel: and the Holy Ghost was upon him. And it was revealed unto him by the Holy Ghost that he should not see death before he had seen the Lord's Christ. And he came by the Spirit into the temple and when the parents had brought in the child Jesus to do for Him according to the custom of the law, He took Him in his arms and blessed God and said "Lord now lettest thou thy servant depart in peace, according to thy word for mine eyes have seen they salvation which thou has prepared before the face of all people, a light to the Gentiles and the glory of thy people Israel." Luke 2 vs 25-32. NKJV

"Also, there was a prophetess named Anna of the tribe of Asher who also spoke of the significance of Jesus' birth." Luke 2 vs 36-38. NKJV

Jesus in His life time also affirmed the prophecies that were written of Him. "You search the scriptures for in them you think you have eternal life, and these are they which testify of Me." John 5 vs 39. NKJV

In His life on earth, Jesus foretold of His death that occurred at age 33 and stated that He would rise from the dead after three days. In Christianity all this came to pass. The Apostle Paul, a Jew who persecuted Christians and was transformed by Jesus, writes: "Moreover, brethren I declare the gospel which I preached to you which also you received and in which you stand, by which also you are saved if you hold fast that word which I preached to you unless you believe in vain. For I delivered to you first of all that which I received that Christ died according to the scriptures, and that He was buried and that He rose again the third day according to the scriptures and that He was seen by Cephas, then by the twelve (apostles)." 1 Corinthians 15 vs 1-5. NKJV

Make Jesus your Lord and Savior

Certain Promises

1

After Jesus was crucified, was resurrected and had returned to earth to show the disciples that He was indeed risen He instructed them on the power of the Holy Spirit, that the helper (the Holy Spirit) would soon be with them.

It was soon after He had ascended—"while they watched He was taken up, and a cloud received Him out of their sight. And while they looked steadfastly toward heaven as He went up, behold, two men stood by them in white apparel, and said to them, 'Men of Galilee why do you stand gazing up into heaven? This same Jesus who was taken up from you into heaven, will so come in like manner as you saw Him go into heaven.'" Acts 1 vs 9-11. NKJV

2

The 12 disciples were not mere followers but actual believers in Jesus and were "eyewitnesses of His majesty". 2 Peter 1 vs 16. NKJV

Jesus told His disciples and those who believe in Him that He would return for believers and followers. "Let not your heart be troubled, you believe in God believe also in Me. In My Father's house are many mansions, if it were not so I would have told you, I go to prepare a place for you and if I go to prepare a place for you, I will come again and receive you to Myself, that where I am, there you may be also." John 14 vs 1-3. NKJV. "You have heard Me say to you, 'I am going away and coming back to you.'" John 14 vs 28. NKJV

3

"For the Lord himself will descend from heaven with a shout with the voice of the archangel and with the trumpet of God and the dead in Christ will rise first. Then we who are alive and remain shall be caught up together with Them in the clouds to meet the Lord in the air. And thus shall we always be with the Lord." 1 Thessalonians 4 vs 16-17. NKJV

4

"So Christ was offered once to bear the sins of many. To those who eagerly await for Him He will appear a second time, apart from sin, for salvation." Hebrews 9 vs 28. NKJV

"And behold I am coming quickly and My reward is with Me to give to every one according to his works. I am the Alpha and the Omega, the Beginning and the End, the First and the Last." Revelation 22 vs 12-13. NKJV

"Behold He is coming with the clouds and every eye shall see him even they who pierced Him, and all the tribes of the earth will mourn because of Him." Revelation 1 vs 7. NKJV

Make Jesus your Lord and Savior

Make Jesus your Lord and Savior

How can you make Jesus your Lord and Savior?

"If you confess with your mouth the Lord Jesus and believe in your heart that God has raised Him from the dead you will be saved. For with the heart one believes unto righteousness and with the mouth confession is made unto salvation. For the scripture says whoever believes on Him will not be put to shame. For there is no distinction between Jew and Greek, for the same Lord over all is rich to all who call upon Him. For whoever calls on the name of the Lord shall be saved." Romans 10 verses 9-13. NKJV

"For God so loved the world that He gave His only begotten Son that whoever believes in Him should not perish but have everlasting life. For God did not send His Son to condemn the world but that the world through Him might be saved." John 3 Vs 16 & 17. NKJV

You are so loved! Ask the Holy Spirt, the third part of the Trinity to help you to make Jesus your Lord and Savior. "But the natural man receiveth not the things of the Spirit of God: for they are foolishness unto Him: neither can He know them, because they are spiritually discerned." 1 Corinthians 2 vs 14. NKJV

Make Jesus your Lord and Savior

"This I say then, Walk in the Spirit, and ye shall not fulfil the lust of the flesh. For the flesh lusteth against the Spirit, and the Spirit against the flesh: and these are contrary the one to the other: so that ye cannot do the things that ye would." Galatians 5 vs 16-17. KJV

I beg you, make Jesus your Lord and Savior for He is coming back. Get ready!

AFTERWORD

"But of that day and hour knoweth no man, no, not the angels of heaven, but my Father only. But as the days of Noah were so shall also the coming of the Son of Man be. For as in the days that were before the flood they were eating and drinking, marrying and giving in marriage until the day that Noah entered into the Ark, and knew not until the flood came, and took them all away; so shall also the coming of the Son of Man be." Matthew 24 vs 36-39 NKJV

"There was a certain rich man who clothed himself in purple and fine linen, and who feasted luxuriously every day. At his gate lay a certain poor man named Lazarus who was covered with sores. Lazarus longed to eat the crumbs that fell from the rich man's table. Instead, dogs would come and lick his sores. The poor man died and was carried by angels to Abraham's side. The rich man also died and was buried. While being tormented in the place of the dead, he looked up and saw Abraham at a distance with Lazarus at his side. He shouted, 'Father Abraham, have mercy on me. Send Lazarus to dip the tip of his finger in water and cool my tongue, because I'm suffering in this flame.' But Abraham said, 'Child, remember that during your lifetime you received good things, whereas Lazarus received terrible things. Now Lazarus is being comforted and you are

Make Jesus your Lord and Savior

in great pain. Moreover, a great crevasse has been fixed between us and you. Those who wish to cross over from here to you cannot. Neither can anyone cross from there to us.' "The rich man said, 'Then I beg you, Father, send Lazarus to my father's house. I have five brothers. He needs to warn them so that they don't come to this place of agony.' Abraham replied, 'They have Moses and the Prophets. They must listen to them.' The rich man said, 'No, Father Abraham! But if someone from the dead goes to them, they will change their hearts and lives.' Abraham said, 'If they don't listen to Moses and the Prophets, then neither will they be persuaded if someone rises from the dead." Luke 16 vs 19-31. CEB

"Nevertheless we, according to His promise, look for new heavens and a new earth in which righteousness dwells." 2 Peter 3 vs 13. NKJV

"Jesus is Coming Back. Get Ready!"

Make Jesus your Lord and Savior

Printed in the United States
by Baker & Taylor Publisher Services